Illustrated
COMPENDIUM
of ANIMALS

Virginie
Aladjidi

Emmanuelle
Tchoukriel

W
FRANKLIN WATTS
LONDON•SYDNEY

INTRODUCTION

Welcome to this *Illustrated Compendium of Animals*. Emmanuelle Tchoukriel is a painter-illustrator trained in medical and scientific illustration. She has drawn the animals in this book with the precision and skill of the naturalist explorers of previous centuries. Before the invention of photography (around 1830), naturalists drew dead or stuffed animals, and brought them to life on paper. Their pictures were printed in books using stone or metal plates to beautiful effect. Emmanuelle Tchoukriel has called her illustrations "plates" as well. She has drawn her 65 plates by either observing the living creatures, or using many photographs. She used a rotring nib and Indian ink to draw the black outlines, and coloured them using watercolours, which sometimes give a translucent effect.

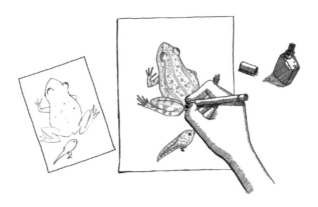 

In this compendium, the animals selected are grouped according to habitat. The tropical rainforest, desert and ocean plates feature animals from around the world. However, the temperate mountain, temperate forest, waterside, town, park and garden and farm plates mainly show animals from Europe. The animals of the savannah are all found in the grasslands of Africa. The Polar regions refer to the Arctic and Antarctic regions around the North and South Poles.

Within these habitats, we have used the scientific method of classification to identify different types of life. In the first instance, scientists pick out two broad groups called "phylum": vertebrates, such as mammals, which have a spine (or vertebral column), and on the other, the invertebrates, such as insects, which do not. Each of these groups is itself divided into several groups called "classes", sometimes with a "subphylum" in between. But it should be noted that the classification of the animals evolves as new discoveries are made, and scientists do not always agree how an animal should be grouped. For example, crustacea used to be viewed as a class of invertebrate but are now more often said to be a subphylum. In this book, we have given each animal the class or occasionally the subphylum in which it has been placed (as well as the species' scientific name in Latin).

Vertebrates alive today are organised into around ten classes. This book considers the six main groups: mammals, birds, cartilaginous fish, ray-finned fish, amphibians and reptiles. The invertebrates (which represent 95 per cent of animal species!) are spread over many subphylum and classes and we have chosen some amazing examples from across these groups.

The drawings in this book are not all drawn to the same scale. Only the three double pages below show, on the same plate, the animals in proportion to others:

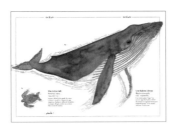
Humpback whale/
leatherback sea turtle
plate 9

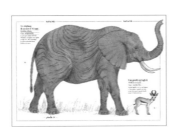
African elephant/springbok
plate 26

giraffe/baby giraffe
plate 31

Certain species in the book have become rare (the tiger, the chimpanzee), some very rare (the black rhinoceros, the Mediterranean monk seal, the leatherback sea turtle), or have even disappeared completely from the wild (the scimitar oryx). We hope this book will inspire its readers to respect and to want to protect these beautiful animals.

CONTENTS

Polar bear

Ursus maritimus

Class: MAMMAL

Giant of the Arctic, the polar
bear blends into the white pack
ice: only his eyes and the tip
of his muzzle are black. His
partially webbed feet make
him a good swimmer.

— *plate 1* —

Emperor penguin

Aptenodytes forsteri

Class: BIRD

These birds are found in the Antarctic. They are the largest species of penguin. Like all penguins, they cannot fly, but swim very well, with their dense feathers and their webbed feet. The male and female emperor penguins greet each other by touching their beaks. It is the male who protects the egg until it hatches.

— *plate 2* —

Snowy (or Arctic) owl

Bubo scandiacus

Class: BIRD

The snowy owl ranges over the Arctic tundra, using its keen eyesight and hearing to find its favourite food, lemmings. Long and thick feathers keep it warm; covering its feet and almost hiding its beak. The female (shown here) has markings in black, whereas the male has completely white feathers.

— *plate 3* —

Arctic fox

Alopex lagopus

Class: MAMMAL

This small fox is well adapted to its Arctic habitat. Its thick fur protects it from the cold and changes from brown to white in winter, so it is camouflaged against the snow. Its small ears and rounded body shape limit heat loss.

— *plate 4* —

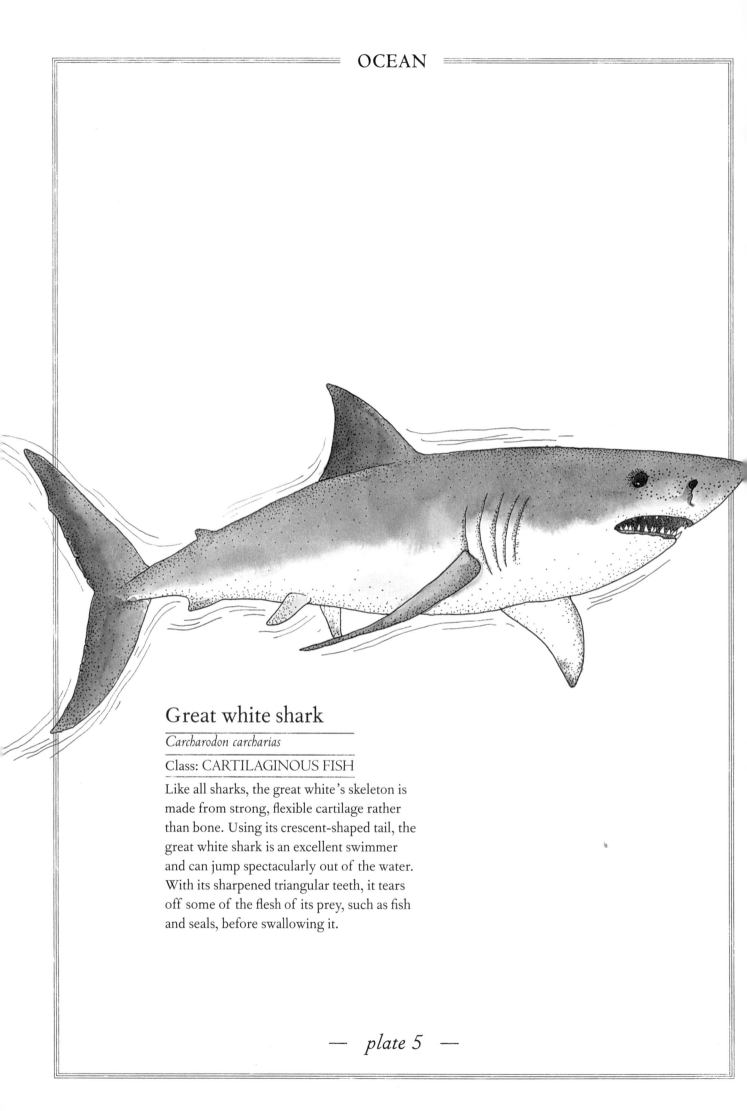

Great white shark

Carcharodon carcharias

Class: CARTILAGINOUS FISH

Like all sharks, the great white's skeleton is made from strong, flexible cartilage rather than bone. Using its crescent-shaped tail, the great white shark is an excellent swimmer and can jump spectacularly out of the water. With its sharpened triangular teeth, it tears off some of the flesh of its prey, such as fish and seals, before swallowing it.

— *plate 5* —

Short-beaked common dolphin

Delphinus delphis

Class: MAMMAL

The dolphin never stops moving (even when asleep!), as it must regularly surface to breathe. Like all mammals, it cannot breathe underwater. Its tapered body and smooth skin make it a remarkable swimmer and it can swim at speeds of over 60 km/h.

— *plate 6* —

Common (or brown) shrimp

Crangon crangon

Subphylum: CRUSTACEAN

It is found in shallow waters near the coast.

fig. 1

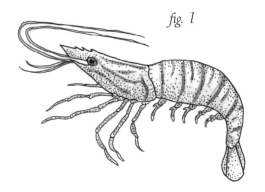

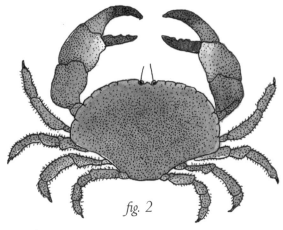

fig. 2

Edible (or brown) crab

Cancer pagurus

Subphylum: CRUSTACEAN

A smooth shell protects its body. It can grow to be over 250 mm wide.

Common octopus

Octopus vulgaris

Class: CEPHALOPOD

It has eight tentacles with suction cups. It can change colour to blend with its surroundings.

fig. 3

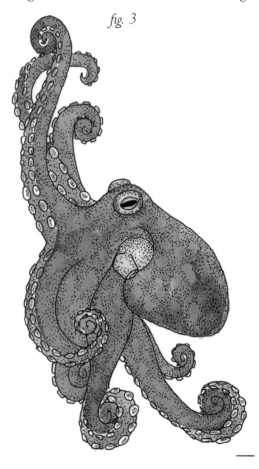

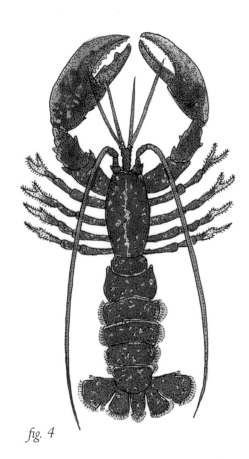

fig. 4

European lobster

Homarus gammarus

Subphylum: CRUSTACEAN

It has ten legs, two with large claws. It hunts for food on the seabed in shallow waters.

— *plate 7* —

Mediterranean monk seal

Monachus monachus

Class: MAMMAL

The fur of the male monk seal is dark brown with a white mark over the stomach. Its fur reminded people of a monk's robes, giving it its name. It loves to eat fish. It is a species threatened with extinction: there were fewer than 450 left in the world in 2015.

— *plate 8* —

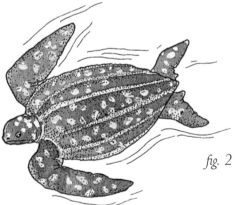

fig. 2

Leatherback sea turtle

Dermochelys coriacea

Class: REPTILE

The leatherback sea turtle is the largest of all turtles and holds the record for long distance swimming (travelling thousands of kilometres through the oceans in search of jellyfish to eat). Its elongated shell has five ribs.

— *plate 9* —

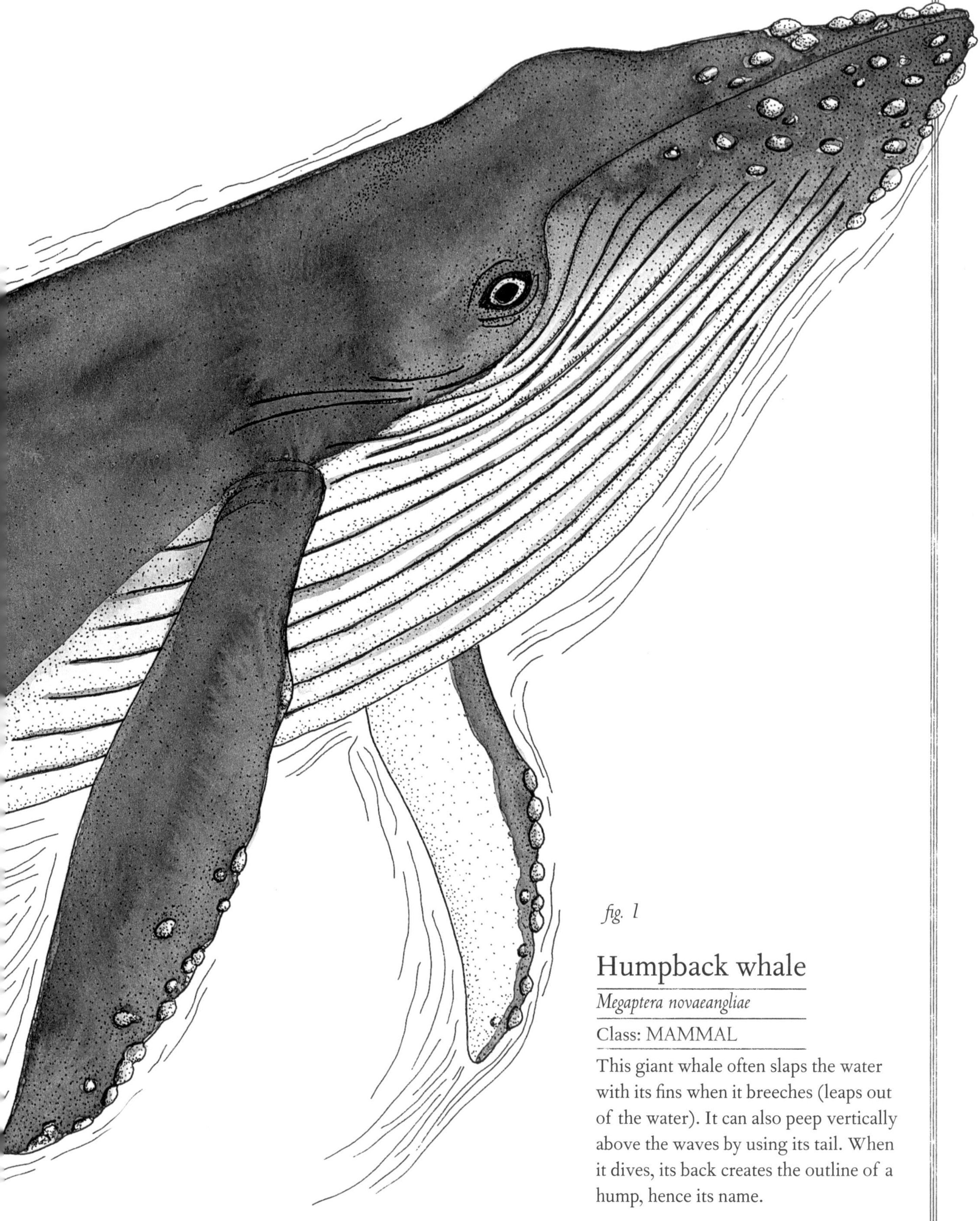

fig. 1

Humpback whale

Megaptera novaeangliae

Class: MAMMAL

This giant whale often slaps the water with its fins when it breeches (leaps out of the water). It can also peep vertically above the waves by using its tail. When it dives, its back creates the outline of a hump, hence its name.

Sea otter
and its pup

Enhydra lutris

Class: MAMMAL

The sea otter is the smallest sea
mammal. Its very dense, thick and
waterproof fur means the otter can
live in cold water. It often floats on
its back, particularly when it sleeps
or to protect its young pup on its
stomach.

— *plate 10* —

Mauve stinger

Pelagia noctiluca

Class: SCYPHOZOA

This jellyfish glows in the dark. It has stinging tentacles.

fig. 1

Common starfish

(or common sea star)

Asterias rubens

Class: ASTEROIDEA

If one of a starfish's five arms is cut off it grows back.

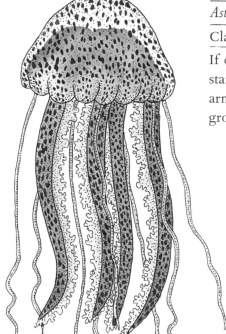

fig. 2

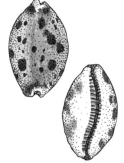

fig. 3

Great scallop

Pecten maximus

Class: BIVALVE

Its shell protects the animal inside. The shell opens and shuts to propel it through the water.

fig. 4

Tiger cowrie

Cypraea tigris

Class: GASTROPOD

The cowrie is a type of sea snail found in coral reefs.

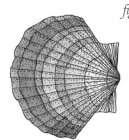

Long-snouted seahorse

Hippocampus guttulatus

Class: RAY-FINNED FISH

The seahorse is a type of bony fish. It is the male that carries the eggs in a stomach pouch.

fig. 5

fig. 6

Red (or precious) coral

Corallium rubrum

Class: ANTHOZOA

The coral is made up of a colony of minute animals.

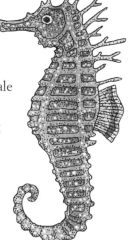

— *plate 11* —

Dyeing dart frog

Dendrobates tinctorius

Class: AMPHIBIAN

fig. 1

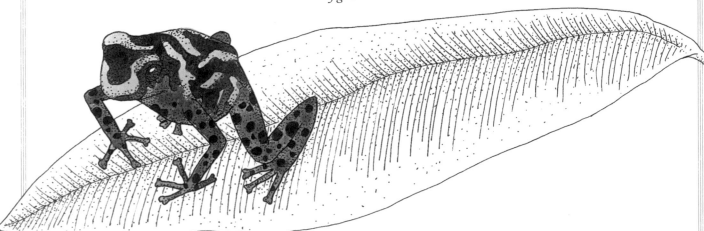

These two species of poison-dart frog are found in the rainforests of South America. Their bright colours warn other animals not to eat them, as their skin produces a deadly poison.

fig. 2

Strawberry poison-dart frog

Dendrobates pumilio

Class: AMPHIBIAN

— *plate 12* —

Pale-throated three-toed sloth

Bradypus tridactylus

Class: MAMMAL

With its arms longer than its legs, the sloth moves around slowly, by day or by night, through the trees of the South American rainforest. It sleeps up to twenty hours a day. Its fur is sometimes greenish as a result of small algae that grow on it. The three-toed sloth is sometimes called an ai because of its high-pitched cry.

— *plate 13* —

Tiger

Panthera tigris

Class: MAMMAL

The tiger, whose coat is fawn with black stripes, is the largest of the big cats. It mainly hunts at night through the forests of Asia. Its stripes help it to blend into the undergrowth. Tigers are an endangered species.

— *plate 14* —

Giant anteater
(or ant bear)

Myrmecophaga tridactyla

Class: MAMMAL

The giant anteater moves between the forests
and more open habitats of South America
in its search for food. It has a long muzzle,
small ears and a thick tail, and walks slowly.
It tears open termite mounds or ants' nests
with the claws of its feet before gathering its
insect meal with its long sticky tongue!

— *plate 15* —

Flap-necked chameleon

Chamaeleo dilepis

Class: REPTILE

This large chameleon, a type of lizard, comes from Africa. A chameleon has eyes that work independently of each other to hunt out its prey. Once it has seen an insect, it swiftly sticks out its long tongue to catch it. Its skin changes colour according to the temperature and its state of health or even according to its mood.

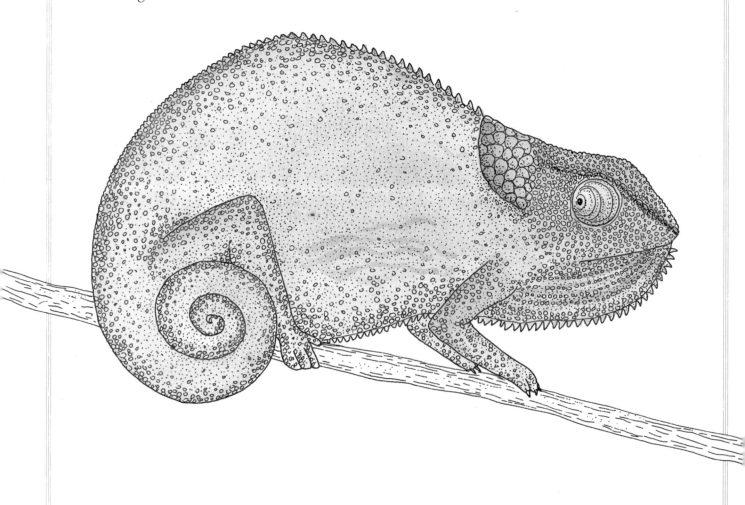

— *plate 16* —

Channel-billed toucan

Ramphastos vitellinus

Class: BIRD

The toucan lives up in the trees of the South American rainforests and cannot fly very well. Its large, long beak is hollow and light. It uses it to eat fruit that has fallen on the ground or occasionally to gulp down eggs, birds and other small animals. When it rains, it opens its beak wide to take a drink.

— *plate 17* —

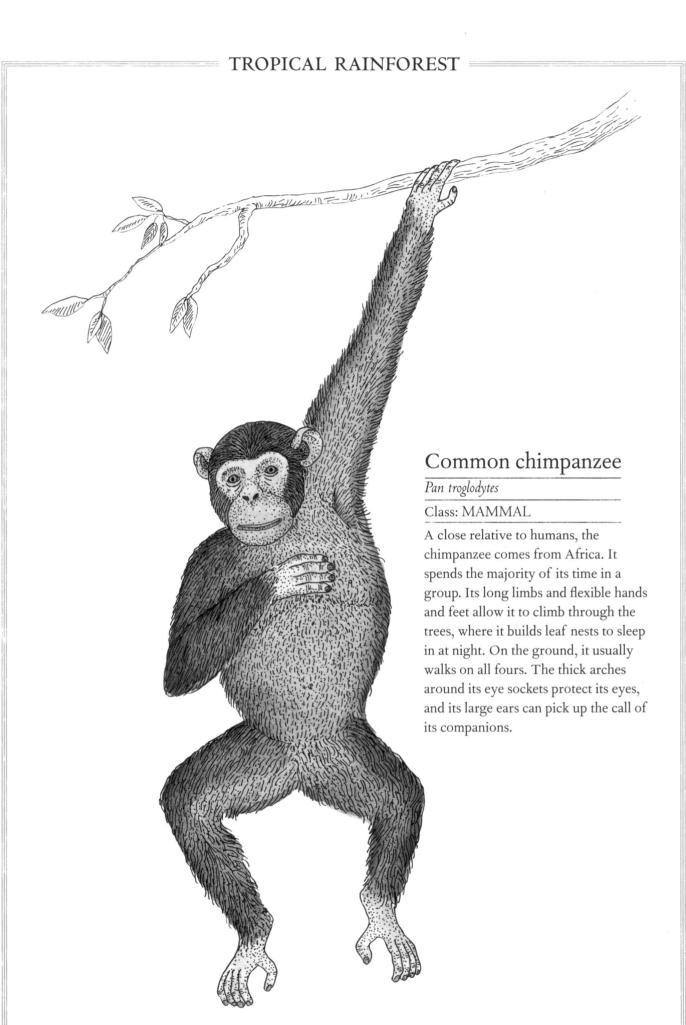

Common chimpanzee

Pan troglodytes

Class: MAMMAL

A close relative to humans, the chimpanzee comes from Africa. It spends the majority of its time in a group. Its long limbs and flexible hands and feet allow it to climb through the trees, where it builds leaf nests to sleep in at night. On the ground, it usually walks on all fours. The thick arches around its eye sockets protect its eyes, and its large ears can pick up the call of its companions.

— *plate 18* —

Smooth-fronted caiman

Paleosuchus trigonatus

Class: REPTILE

This small species of crocodile is found near cool, fast-flowing streams and rivers in the rainforests of South America. Its heavy tail and pointed snout help it swim in fast currents.

— *plate 19* —

Lesser Egyptian jerboa

Jaculus jaculus

Class: MAMMAL

The lesser Egyptian jerboa can make great leaps on its long back legs, like a mini kangeroo, jumping across the sandy and dusty desert. Its tail provides balance. It prefers to leave its burrow in the cool of the desert night.

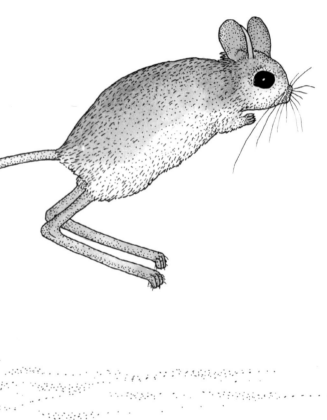

— *plate 20* —

Western diamondbacked rattlesnake

Crotalus atrox

Class: REPTILE

This well-known snake owes its name to the horny rings that make a noise on the end of its tail and the diamond patterns on its scaly skin. It rattles the rings on its tail together to warn off predators in the desert scrub of North America.

fig. 1

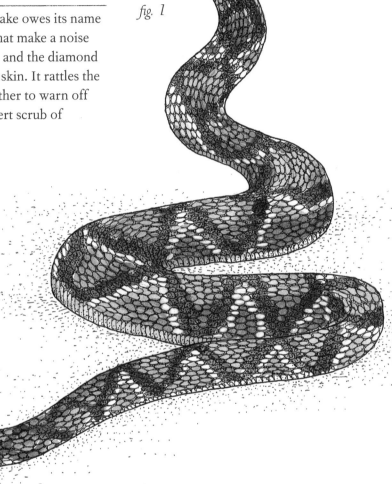

fig. 2

Egyptian sand scorpion

Buthacus arenicola

Class: ARACHNID

The scorpion's exoskeleton is a shell that protects it from drying out. But the animal still spends the day in the shade where it is cooler.

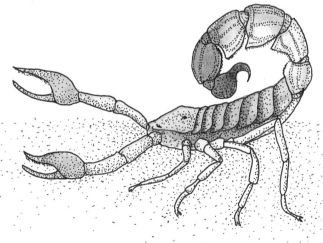

— *plate 21* —

Dromedary (or Arabian camel)

Camelus dromedarius

Class: MAMMAL

The dromedary is known as the "ship of the desert" as it transports people and goods across the deserts of North Africa and the Middle East. It closes its nostrils when it encounters a sandstorm, and its ears and eyes are protected by long hairs. It can survive several days without drinking. Its hump is a fat reserve from which it can produce energy and water.

— *plate 22* —

Scimitar oryx

Oryx dammah

Class: MAMMAL

The oryx's large hooves are perfect for the North African desert. It can survive without water for weeks. This species is extinct in the wild but small herds are still found in special reserves. Some people think its long, ringed horns inspired myths about unicorns.

— *plate 23* —

Ostrich

Struthio camelus

Class: BIRD

The ostrich is the largest of the
bird family. It has long, solid legs
and can run very fast, but cannot
fly. It only has two toes on each
foot, often missing the nail on the
outer toe. It is found in desert and
savannah habitats in Africa.

— *plate 24* —

Fennec fox

Vulpes zerda

Class: MAMMAL

This "sand fox" from North Africa communicates by yapping, like a dog. Its hairy feet prevent it from sinking too far into the sand and protect it from the scorching hot surface. Its large ears lose heat and help keep it cool.

— *plate 25* —

African elephant

Loxodonta africana

Class: MAMMAL

The largest land animal, the elephant crosses great areas of grassland with ease. It can also swim fast. It forages for food with its trunk, using it to carry fruit, leaves and tree bark to its mouth.

fig. 1

— *plate 26* —

Springbok

Antidorcas marsupialis

Class: MAMMAL

Fast and lively on its long and slender legs, this antelope has a supple body and can make great, acrobatic leaps, up to 3 m high.

fig. 2

Lion, a lioness and their cub

Panthera leo

Class: MAMMAL

Lions are fast and agile hunters. These large predators are top of the food chain in the savannah. Their jaws are powerful and their claws sharp and retractable. The lion is distinguishable from the lioness as it has a bigger skull and a thick mane.

— plate 27 —

Leopard

Panthera pardus

Class: MAMMAL

This species of big cat's coat is generally light
yellow, dotted with dark patches. But there
are also individual animals that are very dark,
and are known as "black panthers". Using its
muscular shoulders and front legs, the leopard
often pulls itself up into the trees in order to
eat its prey or to rest.

— *plate 28* —

Red-billed oxpecker

Buphagus erythrorhynchus

Class: BIRD

The oxpecker rides on the back of large mammals. It eats parasites found on them or feeds on the blood from a wound.

fig. 1

fig. 2

Black rhinoceros

Diceros bicornis

Class: MAMMAL

In the dry savannah, the rhinoceros often bathes in the mud in order to stay cool and ward off parasites. Its very thick skin is almost hairless. The rhino is critically endangered as people hunt it for its horn, which is thought by some to have medicinal value.

— *plate 29* —

Plains zebra

Equus quagga

Class: MAMMAL

The zebra grazes from dawn to dusk, and sleeps standing up. It has a long narrow head and large ears. No two zebras have exactly the same pattern of stripes.

— *plate 30* —

Giraffe
and its offspring
(or calf)

Giraffa camelopardalis

Class: MAMMAL

fig. 1

The giraffe is a graceful giant with a long neck. Its front legs are longer than the hind ones so its back is sloped. It grows to over 5 m tall allowing it to graze on the leaves of the acacia tree which are beyond the reach of other grazing animals.

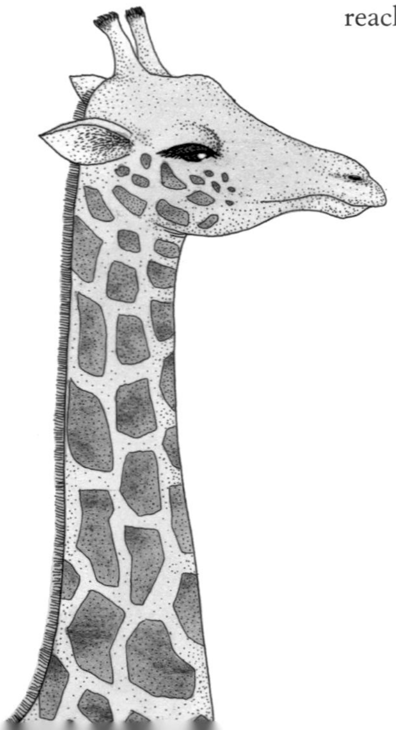

fig. 2

Straight from birth the young giraffe resembles its parents: it is like an adult in miniature (but is only 2 m tall). Mothers and offspring live in a group.

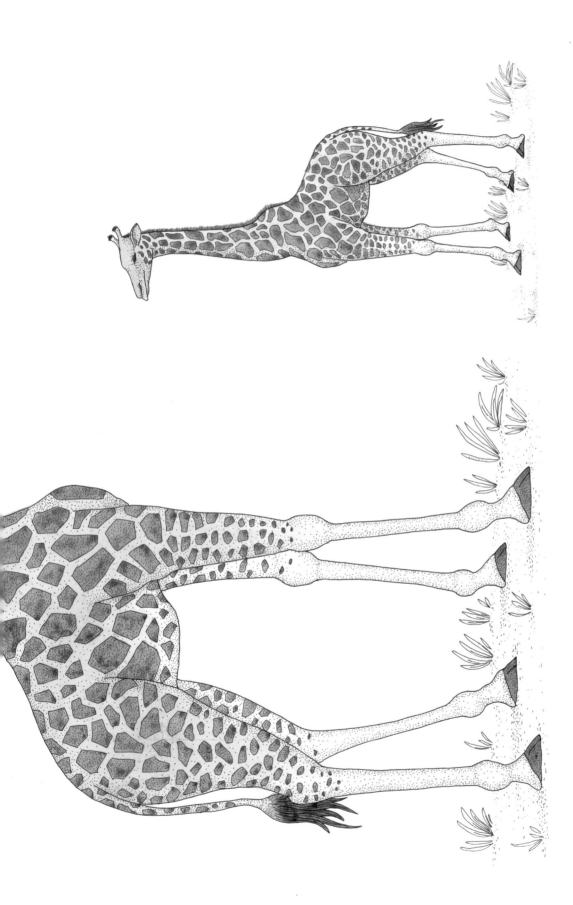

— *plate 31* —

Alpine marmot

Marmota marmota

Class: MAMMAL

The marmot is a rodent that lives in the mountains of central and southern Europe. It never strays far from its burrow and stands on its hind legs to observe the surrounding area. If it spots danger, it lets out a loud whistle to warn other marmots.

— *plate 32* —

Golden eagle

Aquila chrysaetos

Class: BIRD

With its long wings, the golden eagle can glide for hours, ranging over an area as large as 200 km². It uses its hooked claws, known as talons, to catch its prey, which includes marmots, rabbits, snakes or roe deer. It tears its food apart with its hooked beak.

— *plate 33* —

Grey wolf

Canis lupus

Class: MAMMAL

The grey wolf has large pointed teeth, a long muzzle, and powerful long, clawed legs. This hunter howls to announce its presence and to defend its territory. Once common throughout Europe, the grey wolf is now found in more remote wilderness and mountain areas.

— *plate 34* —

Weasel

Mustela nivalis

Class: MAMMAL

The weasel has a head that is barely wider than its neck, so it can access mouse holes and the burrows of other small rodents it likes to eat. The weasel, with its short tail, also climbs trees in order to steal from nests. It lives in forest, woods and hedgerows as well as mountain habitats.

— *plate 35* —

Rock ptarmigan
(or snow partridge)

Lagopus mutus

Class: BIRD

The ptarmigan, a stocky bird with small rounded wings and a short beak, has solid feet covered in feathers which act as "snow shoes" in the soft snow. White in winter, it becomes almost entirely grey-brown in summer. It can be found in the mountains but also in northern polar regions.

— *plate 36* —

Chamois

Rupicapra rupicapra

Class: MAMMAL

The chamois is a type of mountain goat. It is an agile climber; it can make leaps 2 m high and 6 m in length over rocky hillsides. Its horn ends are hooked backwards.

— *plate 37* —

Red deer

Cervus elaphus

Class: MAMMAL

Red deer are found in the woods, forests and open moors of Europe. The male stag grows antlers each spring, which fall off the following winter. Stags sometimes clash antlers when they compete for female mates. A red deer is reddish brown during the summer and grey-brown in the winter, when its fur is thicker.

— plate 38 —

Red squirrel

Sciurus vulgaris

Class: MAMMAL

The red squirrel's bushy tail is as long as its body. The squirrel climbs and jumps, feeding on the ground or in the trees, and holds its food, hazelnuts, fir cones or eggs, for example, with its front paws. Red squirrels are found across Europe but are now rare in Britain, losing territory to the more common grey squirrel.

— *plate 39* —

Great spotted cuckoo

Clamator glandarius

Class: BIRD

This cuckoo visits southern Europe and western Asia in the summer, migrating to Africa in the winter. It flies about with other cuckoos and hops on the ground, with its tail raised. It lays its eggs in other birds' nests, and, not noticing the addition, these birds then feed the cuckoo chick when it hatches.

— *plate 40* —

fig. 1

European hedgehog

Erinaceus europaeus

Class: MAMMAL

The hedgehog has around 7,000 prickly bristles which stand on end when it defends itself from predators. It can roll into a ball to protect itself too. It is found in hedges or gardens as well as woods and forests.

Burgundy (or Roman) snail

Helix pomatia

Class: GASTROPOD

In the grass at the forest edge, the snail inches forward, sliding along on a trail of slime given out by its muscly foot.

fig. 2

— *plate 41* —

Wild boar sow and her piglets

Sus scrofa

Class: MAMMAL

Despite its squat frame and its short legs, the wild boar can run fast, and is also a strong swimmer. The female, the sow, lives in a group with her piglets.

fig. 1

fig. 2

The piglet has pale markings across its back, allowing it to camouflage itself in its nest of leaves. Wild boar became extinct in Britain a long time ago but they are being reintroduced to some forest areas.

— *plate 42* —

Red fox

Vulpes vulpes

Class: MAMMAL

This fox's coat is generally red, sometimes brown-grey; its long tail is bushy. The fox is light on its feet. It shelters and raises its cubs in a den. As well as woods and forests, the red fox has adapted to living in towns and cities.

— *plate 43* —

fig. 1

Western honey bee

Apis mellifera

Class: INSECT

Honey bees live is social groups that are made up of more than 40,000 bees.

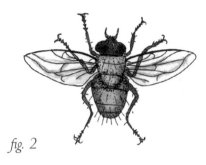

fig. 2

Green bottle fly

Lucilia sericata

Class: INSECT

Its shiny body is protected by tiny bristles.

fig. 3

Seven-spotted ladybird

Coccinella septempunctata

Class: INSECT

It is a carnivore and eats around 150 aphids (small green insects) per day.

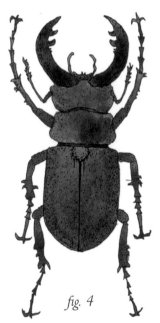

fig. 4

Stag beetle

Lucanus cervus

Class: INSECT

The male has enormous antler-like mandibles that frighten off its enemies.

fig. 5

Jet black ant

Lasius fuliginosus

Class: INSECT

In order to find its way around, it follows the scent left by fellow ants.

— *plate 44* —

Fire salamander

Salamandra salamandra

Class: AMPHIBIAN

The fire salamander is found in the forests of central and southern Europe. It comes out at night, leaving its cool and damp shelter to feed. The female sets down her larvae in shallow water just after they are born but they leave the water when they become adults as this species of salamander cannot swim.

— plate 45 —

Mallard duck, the female and their duckling

Anas platyrhynchos

Class: BIRD

fig. 1

Mallard ducks have webbed feet which act as oars for swimming, but they can also fly. During the mating season, the male has a green head with a yellow beak and a white collar. The rest of the time it is more brown in colour.

fig. 3

The duckling waterproofs its feathers at a very young age with an oil it secretes and spreads over its feathers using its beak.

fig. 2

The female mallard duck has brown plumage and beige spots.

— *plate 46* —

Mute swan and its cygnet

Cygnus olor

Class: BIRD

The adult swan, with its long flexible neck, has white plumage, a black area at the base of its red-orange beak, and black legs and feet. The swan can fly very well despite its weight, building up speed before take off by running across the water. It sometimes carries its young, called cygnets, on its back.

— *plate 47* —

Common kingfisher

Alcedo atthis

Class: BIRD

fig. 1

The common kingfisher lives by the banks of clean, shallow streams and rivers. To catch fish, it dives head first into the water, its wings stretched back.

fig. 2

The kingfisher beats its wings to leave the water with its catch. Once it has landed, it knocks the fish unconscious before swallowing it.

— *plate 48* —

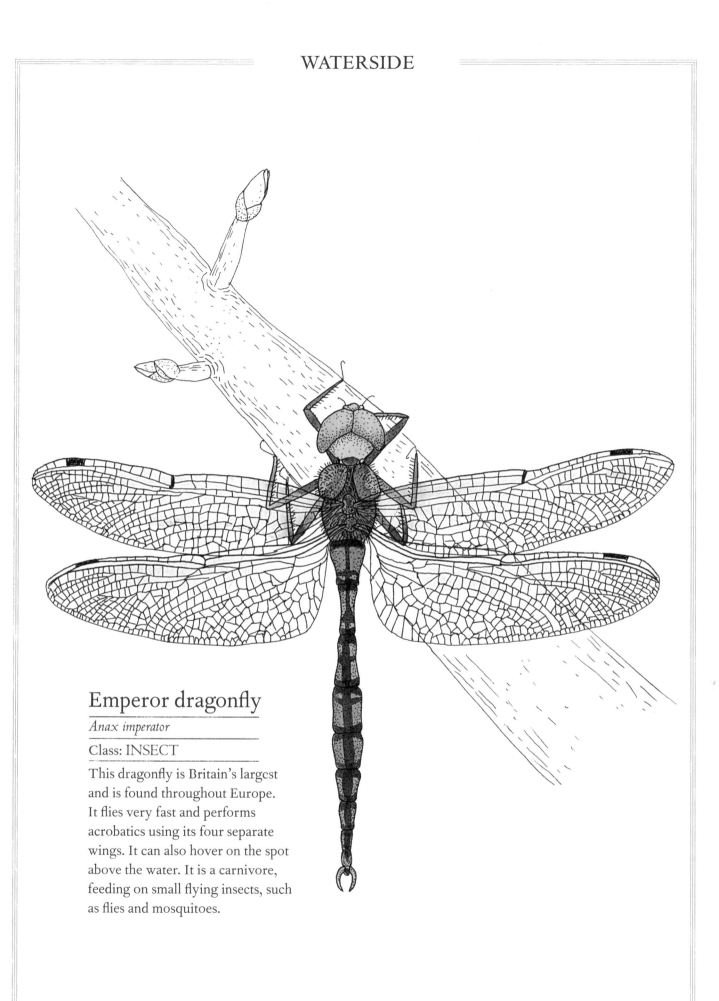

Emperor dragonfly

Anax imperator

Class: INSECT

This dragonfly is Britain's largest and is found throughout Europe. It flies very fast and performs acrobatics using its four separate wings. It can also hover on the spot above the water. It is a carnivore, feeding on small flying insects, such as flies and mosquitoes.

— *plate 49* —

Grey heron

Ardea cinerea

Class: BIRD

This bird is the largest type of heron in Europe. It walks delicately on its long legs in shallow waters. At the slightest movement in the water, it stretches its neck a little, then, in a flash, stabs and captures a fish or a frog with its powerful beak.

— *plate 50* —

Edible frog and its tadpole

Rana esculenta

Class: AMPHIBIAN

The frog's back legs are strong, for jumping. The frog does not drink through its mouth, but absorbs water through its smooth skin so it needs to keep damp.

fig. 1

fig. 2

Frogs lay their eggs in water. The tadpoles hatch from these, living underwater and breathing with gills. As they grow they change, or metamorphise, into adult frogs, developing lungs which allow them to breathe air and live on land. The back legs have already formed on this tadpole; its front ones will grow and its tail will disappear. It will then leave the water as a small version of its parents.

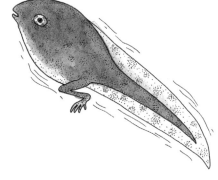

— *plate 51* —

Alpine newt

Ichthyosaura alpestris

Class: AMPHIBIAN

The alpine newt is seen on the ground in hilly areas, sheltered in cool, damp places. But it spends a lot of its time in the water, particularly in spring during the mating season, when the male newts, like this one, develop spectacular colours. The rest of the year they are brown.

— *plate 52* —

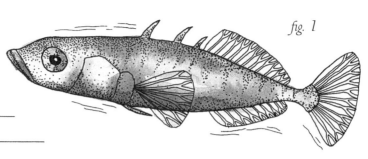

fig. 1

Three-spined stickleback
(male and female)

Gasterosteus aculeatus

Class: RAY-FINNED FISH

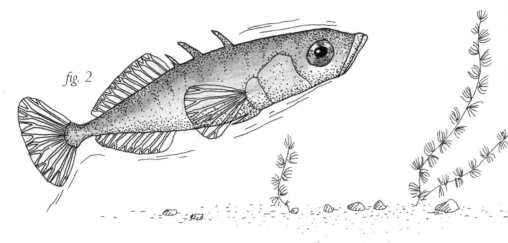

fig. 2

In spring, the male stickleback displays his stomach, that has turned red, to attract the silver and green female, so that she can lay eggs in the nest he has built at the bottom of the river lake or pond.

Northern pike

Esox lucius

Class: RAY-FINNED FISH

The pike is a large, freshwater predator with 700 sharp teeth. With its single dorsal fin, the pike is very fast. It camouflages itself in the water weeds with the help of the light stripes on its body, before surprising its prey.

fig. 3

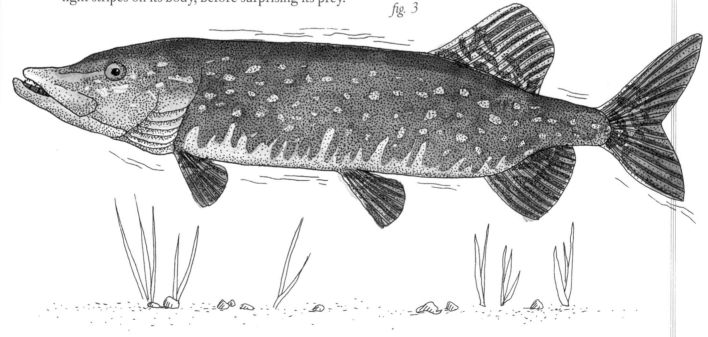

— *plate 53* —

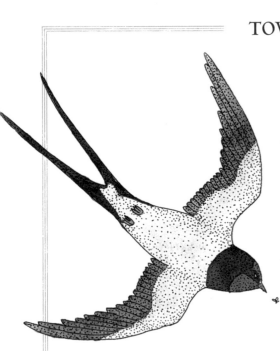

Swallow

Hirundo rustica

Class: BIRD

The swallow feeds
on insects as it flies.
It migrates to warm
countries during the
winter.

fig. 1

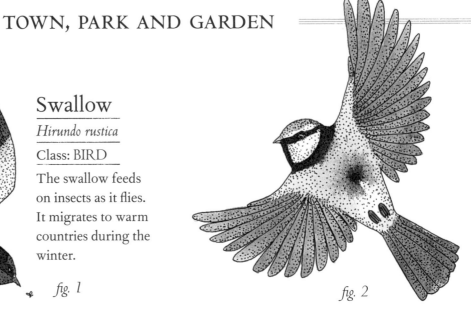

fig. 2

Blue tit

Parus caeruleus

Class: BIRD

The female blue tit lays 8 to 12
eggs in its nest and sits on them
until they hatch. Both parents
feed their chicks.

Eurasian collared dove

Streptopelia decaocto

Class: BIRD

The dove's characteristic call
(a repeated coo-coo-coo)
can be heard from early
spring onwards.

fig. 3

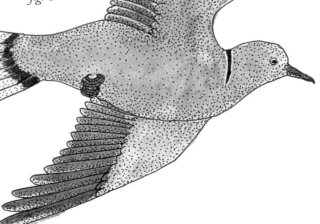

fig. 4

House sparrow

Passer domesticus

Class: BIRD

The sparrow lives close to humans,
almost everywhere on Earth.

— *plate 54* —

Stone (or beech) marten

Martes foina

Class: MAMMAL

The stone marten is native to Europe and Asia but is not found in Britain. It has a white throat and a bushy tail. In the town, it goes through bins to find food. It sometimes shelters in attics or under car bonnets.

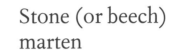

— *plate 55* —

fig. 1

Red admiral

butterfly

Vanessa atalanta

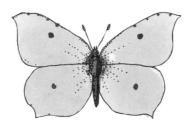

fig. 2

Common brimstone

butterfly

Gonepteryx rhamni

fig. 3

Orange tip

butterfly

Anthocharis cardamines

fig. 4

Wall brown

butterfly

Lasiommata megera

fig. 5

Swallowtail

butterfly

Papilio machaon

Butterflies

Lepidoptera

Class: INSECT

The wings and the body of the butterfly are covered in tiny scales. Butterflies bask in the sun, absorbing its heat through their wings to give them the energy to fly and feed.

fig. 6

Peacock butterfly

Inachis io

fig. 7

Small tortoiseshell

butterfly

Aglais urticae

fig. 8

Large (or cabbage)

white butterfly

Pieris brassicae

fig. 9

Common blue

butterfly

Polyommatus icarus

The caterpillar of the swallowtail

Papilio machaon

Class: INSECT

fig. 10

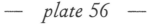

A caterpillar hatches from a butterfly's egg. It feeds on plants and grows, until it forms a chrysalis, a kind of case, around itself. Inside, it changes into an adult butterfly and emerges from the chrysalis to spread its wings.

— *plate 56* —

Domestic cat

Felis catus

Class: MAMMAL

The cat is a formidable hunter in our gardens. It walks on the front of its padded feet, effectively on tip toe, giving it silent, flexible movement. In the twilight, the pupils of its eyes enlarge and become round, and it can see well enough to hunt.

— *plate 57* —

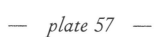

Black-headed gull

Larus ridibundus

Class: BIRD

The black-headed gull lives near water, such as the ponds in parks. Its Latin name means the laughing gull, on account of its noisy cry, which sounds a little like laughter. A black-headed gull's head is, in fact, mainly white in winter and dark brown in the summer.

— *plate 58* —

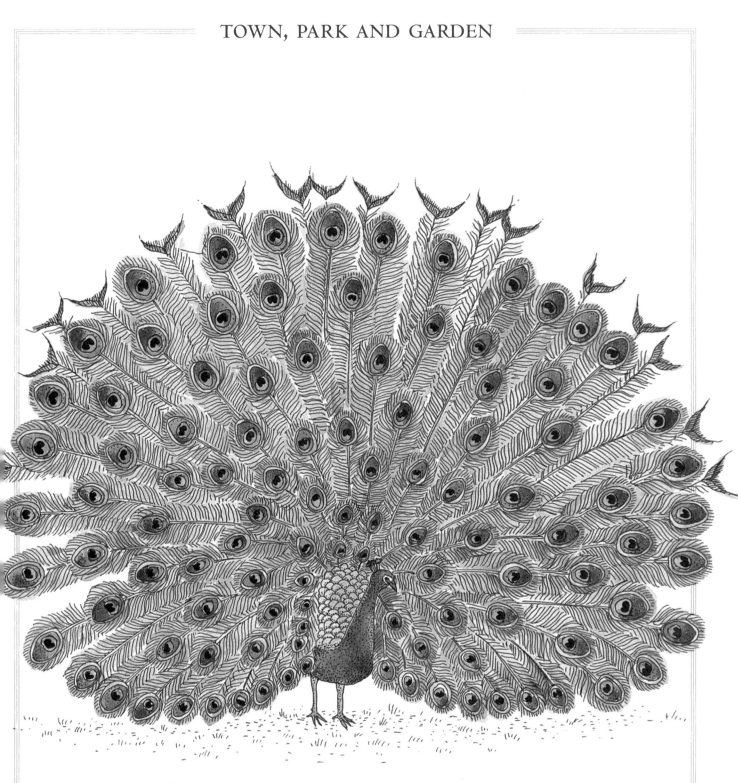

Indian peafowl

Pavo cristatus

Class: BIRD

The male peacock's tail feathers stand up like a fan in order to impress the female peahen. Each feather in the tail finishes with an eyespot (a marking which resembles an eye), in very vibrant colours. It originated in Asia but people brought these beautiful birds to Europe where they add colour to parks and gardens.

— *plate 59* —

Chicken (chick, hen and cock)

Gallus gallus

Class: BIRD

Chickens fly very little and peck at the ground searching for seeds or worms. The male cock and female hen mate, fertilising the eggs. The hen lays her eggs in a nest and sits on them until the chicks hatch out. Hens also lay unfertilised eggs which people eat.

— *plate 60* —

Pig

Sus domesticus

Class: MAMMAL

Farmers keep pigs for meat.
The pig has a body shaped like
a barrel, slender legs and a large
head. Its snout, much like a
bulldozer, helps it root out food.
This is a sow, a female pig.

— *plate 61* —

Sheep
and its lamb

Ovis aries

Class: MAMMAL

Farmers keep sheep for wool, milk and meat. There are over 200 breeds of sheep. In some breeds, only the males (rams) have horns, in others the females (ewes) have them as well. This is a black-faced ewe with her lamb.

— *plate 62* —

Domestic goat

Capra hircus

Class: MAMMAL

Farmers keep goats for their meat and milk, which is good for making cheese. With its hooves, the goat can forage on steep hillsides. It chews on just about anything it can reach, looking for the plants it likes to eat. This is a nanny (female) goat. Her young are called kids.

— *plate 63* —

Cattle

Bos taurus

Class: MAMMAL

Farmers keep cattle for milk and meat.
Cattle ruminate: they eat grass which is
first swallowed without being chewed, then
comes back up out of the stomach to the
mouth for chewing. Then they swallow it
again. Like all mammals, the female (cow)
feeds its offspring – its calf – on milk, which
the calf sucks from its mother's udders.

— *plate 64* —

Donkey (or ass) and its foal

Equus asinus

Class: MAMMAL

fig. 2

The foal is the offspring of the male jack donkey and the female jenny.

fig. 1

The donkey is a type of small horse with large ears and a long tail. Donkeys are often kept as pets but, in some parts of the world, they are used to pull carts and carry loads.

— *plate 65* —

GLOSSARY

algae Simple plants that grow in or near water.

amphibian A class of animals, such as a frog or a newt, that can live both on land and in water.

anthozoa A class of animals that includes sea anemones and corals. Their simple body has an opening surrounded by tentacles.

arachnid A class of animals including spiders, scorpions and mites. Most arachnids have a two-sectioned body and eight legs.

asteroidea A class of spiny marine animals, such as starfish and sea stars.

big cat A large wild animal that belongs to the cat family. Lions, panthers, tigers and leopards are all big cats.

bird A class of animals covered with feathers that has wings and two feet and can usually fly.

bivalve A class of shellfish, such a mussel or an oyster, that has a shell in two parts.

breathe In an animal, to take air in and out of the lungs or, underwater, through the gills.

breed In animals, sexual reproduction to produce young.

camouflage Colour, pattern or shape of an animal's body that allows it to blend into the background and not be noticed.

carnivore An animal that eats mainly meat.

cartilaginous fish A class of fish, including sharks and rays, that have skeletons formed of cartilage rather than bone.

cephalopod A class of animals, including octopus, squid and cuttlefish, that has tentacles and swims by pushing water out of its body.

class In classification, a large group of living things with similar characteristics.

classification In science, the organisation of different living things into categories, starting with a kingdom (such as animals) then breaking this down into smaller and smaller groups.

compendium A collection of information presented clearly but in few words.

crustacean A subphylum of animals with soft bodies divided into sections and a hard outer shell. Most live in water, including crabs.

desert An area of land, usually covered with sand, with little or no water.

exoskeleton A stiff layer on the outside of some invertebrates that protects the soft tissue inside. Insects have exoskeletons.

extinct When a species dies out completely.

fertilise In animals, when a female egg joins with male sperm to start developing a new animal.

gastropod A large and diverse class of animals. Snails and slugs are gastropods.

gills The body organ that fish (and the young of some amphibians) use to breathe.

habitat The natural home or environment where an animal or a plant usually lives.

insect A class of animal with six legs, a three-sectioned body, no backbone and often wings.

insulation A layer, such as animal fat or fur, that helps keeps heat in or out of a body.

invertebrates Animals without backbones, such as insects. The invertebrates form a phylum in the animal kingdom.

larvae The stage in the lifecycle of some animals after it hatches from an egg and before it develops into an adult.

lungs Breathing organs inside an animal's body.

mammal A class of animals that have warm blood, hair or fur. Most give birth to live young and the mothers produce milk to feed them.

mandibles The crushing parts of an insect's mouth.

mate The sexual partner of an animal. Used as a verb, it is the sexual act that forms part of animal reproduction.

mating season The time of the year when animals mate.

migrate When an animal moves from one area or habitat to another, according to the seasons.

parasite A living thing that lives in, or on, another living thing. Ticks, lice and intestinal worms are all parasites.

phylum In classification, the group that comes beneath a kingdom and above a class or subphylum.

plumage The feathers that cover a bird's body.

polar Describes the icy regions of the Earth at the extreme north and south of the planet.

predator An animal that hunts other animals for food.

prey An animal that is hunted and killed for food by another.

ray-finned fish A large and diverse class of fish that are named by their fins, which are formed from bony structures with skin covering them.

reptile A class of animals that have a backbone and are usually cold-blooded, with scaly skin.

rodent A small gnawing mammal, such as a guinea pig, mouse, rat, hamster or squirrel.

savannah A large, flat area of land covered with grass and a few trees, found around or in tropical areas, such as in East Africa.

skeleton A framework of bone or cartilage on the inside or outside of an animal's body that gives structure to an animal.

species A group of animals that can breed together to produce fertile offspring.

subphylum In classification, a category below phylum and above class.

scyphozoa Jellyfish belong to this class of boneless animals that swim freely in the sea.

temperate Describes a region with a mild climate.

tropical rainforest A thick forest in parts of the world where there is almost daily rainfall.

tundra Large flat areas of treeless land in cold areas of the world, such as the Arctic, where the ground is frozen in winter and marshy in summer.

vertebrate Animals that have a backbone, also called a spine. The vertebrates form a phylum in the animal kingdom.

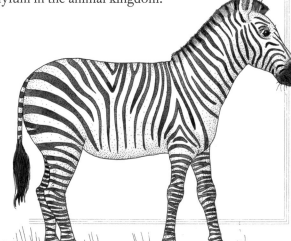

INDEX OF PLATES